30 DAYS ...
SURVIVING THE TRAUMA AND UNEXPECTED LOSS OF A SINGLE PARENT AS AN ONLY CHILD

Kinyatta E. Gray

Written By: Kinyatta E. Gray © 2019
Published By: Pen Legacy®
Cover By: Christian Cuan
Formatting by : www.TheLiarsCraft.com

ALL RIGHTS RESERVED. No part of this book may be reproduced in any written, electronic, recording, or photocopying without written permission of the publisher or author. The exception would be in the case of brief quotations embodied in the critical articles or reviews and pages where permission is specifically granted by the publisher or author.

DISCLAIMER

Although you may find the teachings, life lessons and examples in this book to be useful, the book is sold with the understanding that neither the author nor Pen Legacy® are engaged in presenting any legal, relationship, financial, emotional, or health advice.

Any person who's experiencing financial, anxiety, depression, health, or relationship issues should consult with a licensed therapist, advisor, licensed psychologist, or any qualified professional before commencing into anything described in this book. This book's intent is to provide you with the writer's account and experience with overcoming life matters. All results will differ than yours; however, our goal is to provide you with our "take" on how to overcome and be resilient when faced with circumstances. There are lessons in every blessing.

Library of Congress Cataloging – in- Publication Data has been applied for.

ISBN: 978-1-7333964-3-1
PRINTED IN THE UNITED STATES OF AMERICA.

Table of Contents

Dedication
Acknowledgements
Foreword

Introduction
1

Chapter 1   30 Days and Counting
7

Chapter 2   Parts of Our Lives
13

Chapter 3   Following My Inner Voice
35

Chapter 4   Bye Mommy
41

Chapter 5   Reflecting Back
57

Chapter 6   Love In a Box
61

Dedication

This book is dedicated to my mother Beverly Esther Carroll.

She was enormously proud of the first play she wrote and produced called *"The Great White Throne"* and always had a desire to write and produce other plays and to become a published author.

ACKNOWLEDGMENTS

First, I would like to thank God for blessing me with this writing talent I inherited from my mother.

Next, I could not have ever been able to complete this book without the love, dedication, encouragement, and unwavering support from my loving spouse and best friend, Julie. On so many nights, we barely spoke because I was so focused on completing this book. She was patient, she was kind and she understood. I love you with me whole heart forever.

My children Domo & Dime have always been my rock and my primary motivation to keep pressing forward. They made me a strong and loving woman and I thank them for all the life lessons they have taught me as we navigated life together and in love. I thank God for blessing me with two wonderful and educated children whom I adore more than anything in this world. I love you both through this lifetime and the next.

To my grandson Karter, one day you will read this book and you will understand that you not only were a gift to all of us when we needed you most but because of your life, I also continued living. I love you baby KBT!

Thank you to several friends who answered the call when it seemed like I was not going to be able to write this book and share my story. You all swooped in with valuable information and guidance so that I could fulfill a purpose and complete a mission that's about something much bigger than me. Thank you for helping me to become an author. I will never forget.

Disclaimer: My memory is not perfect and I'm sharing information to the best of my knowledge. Identities have been changed to avoid legal pitfalls.

Foreword

When asked to write this foreword, to this unique and profound work of art by Mrs. Kinyatta Gray, I was flattered but felt it more fitting to call it a forward, as in moving forward. Not just because of the content, but the steps that it took to put this book into context was a huge step towards the direction of healing from a loss that one could never prepare for. It's a book about growth and being uprooted simultaneously from everything that you have ever known. It's about growing up, branching out, and learning about love, life and finding happiness from within.

Mrs. Gray and I met at work and she was having a particularly bothersome morning. Upon introducing myself to her, she seemed less than enthralled to have a member of the team that was super energetic in the morning. I dismissed her lack of energy as her not being a morning person. Later that afternoon, Kinyatta approached me with an apology for her mood during our initial introduction and cited that she wasn't aware that her team had acquired a new member. After admitting that she wasn't her best self when we met, she reintroduced herself as the person that I know today.

From that moment forward, we embarked on a relationship that I was drawn to because of her honesty and candidness about her life, her family and most of all, her relationship and memories of her mother, affectionately known as Miss Bee.

Not only has Kinyatta worked her way to a top tier government position, but also she is the CEO of her business, FlightsInStilettos®. Her love for her family, zest for life and business savviness make this new author a force to be reckoned with.

As you turn each page of this book, you will have the rare opportunity to glimpse into the life of this beautiful being. You will come to learn the struggles and path that she took to achieve and maintain her brand of happiness. It will leave you spellbound and wanting to learn more about Mrs. Kinyatta Gray and her future successes that follow.

Peace and Blessings,
Dr. Jamilah

Introduction

I never thought about becoming an author until now. My mother, Beverly E. Carroll was a literary genius.

Without a doubt, my talents come from her and I am writing this book to honor my mother.

I was born and raised in the Washington, D.C. area.

Over the years, I've made quite a name for myself. Known for my love of fashion and style, I launched a business in 2018 called FlightsInStilettos® that focuses on inspiring women to put their best selves forward when traveling. My brand has been spotted around the world and supported by a vast number of celebrities.

I grew up as an only child; raised by my doting and loving mother. For most of my life, she raised me as a single mother. She was the only authority figure I knew and respected.

During my formative years, my mom worked as a nanny caring for the children of affluent attorneys; while ironically, I was cared for by a babysitter in the inner city.

Occasionally, she'd take me to work with her and I'd get to play with toys that were better than mine and eat fancier food. One of the meals I enjoyed eating was tuna melts. Damn, the cheese those attorneys had was so much better!

My babysitter was a kind lady who had an adult son at home who would play Teddy Pendergrass records during the day. I grew to love Teddy Pendergrass.

The babysitter cared for several other kids during the day, but I was her favorite. She loved my long ponytails and my sweet and respectful disposition. She'd occasionally make rice pudding and set a bowl aside just for me.

I was well taken care of, but not as well as the kids my mom cared for. She took them to swimming classes and ballet and all I got to do was play hopscotch and jump rope on cracked cement in the inner city.

One time when playing on the cracked cement I fell face forward and cracked my two front teeth.

My mom worked hard and faithfully to take care of me. I was always well dressed and groomed and my teachers would always tell her that. My mom took pride in taking exceptional care of me.

One time she took me to get my pictures taken and because of my looks and grooming my picture became a marketing tool for the picture company.

My momma was a church-going woman who tried her best to live a holy and God-fearing life.

She was in at least three choirs and would catch taxicabs or the bus to and from rehearsals during the weeknights... that's if we didn't get rides home from the deacons. I remember riding in the back of the deacon's Cadillac relieved I didn't have to stand up on the bus.

Throughout the years my mom and I developed a strong and unbreakable bond and close mother/daughter relationship.

All of my love, emotional support and affirmation came from her and no one else. Nor did I expect it from anyone else.

She instilled my values and my God-fearing ways. She was truly all that I had in life —- that was solid, stable and true. I only trusted her.

Over the years, my life would mimic many of the same oppressing challenges she faced during her life.

Generational curses are real. You must recognize them and break them.

After experiencing a series of unforeseen traumatic events over the years and more specifically in 2018, I feel compelled to share with you that you must be in tune with and follow your inner voice.

Your inner voice is your spirit guide speaking to you and giving you direction and guidance.

As you read this book, I will take you on an emotional and riveting journey and give you an up-close and personal glimpse into my often-secretive life.

I hope that you will read this book and never look at 30-days that same way again.

30 Days and Counting

September 21, 2018, started like any other day; work as usual. I appreciate my steady paycheck, but Lord knows that I am destined to do more with my life and my creative gifts. I have spent a lot of time strategizing and thinking about what it would be like to take my brand, FlightsInStilettos®, to the next level. In doing so, this was my daily mental escape from a rather mundane and predictable workday.

My mom was my biggest supporter of FlightsInStilettos® (FIS). Her unwavering support came with lavish perks such as being the first to know about and receive all my new products. Every time I launched a new product, I relied heavily on her feedback about the likelihood of its success.

She believed in me and my business so much that she encouraged me to reach out to celebrities for product endorsements.

Many celebrities answered the call and have been spotted all over the world with many of my products. I'm so glad that I took my mom's advice.

In spite of these accomplishments, my workdays at my 9 to 5 continued to drag on. I made the best of it and gave my all to my work assignments, although my heart was truly with my 1st love, FlightsInStilettos®.

Every single morning on my way to work, it was a sacred ritual to call my mother, whom I affectionately refer to as "My Miss Bee". We'd both use that opportunity to motivate each other so that we could get through our workdays. We'd also use that time to catch up on the current news of our closest friends. Some would call it "gossip"; I call it "daily briefings". LOL. Every single conversation included me bouncing ideas off her about FlightsInStilettos®. I knew she was sick of hearing about it, but I didn't care; she's my momma and she's supposed to listen to my babbling.

I also shared more with my mom than anyone else, and she did the same because we knew intrinsically that we were each other's solely trusted best friend.

We'd laugh and laugh and sigh and wish things were different as we both pulled up to our jobs; I'd talk to my mom up until the last possible moment. As my car approached the garage at work, I'd talk to her until the connection was lost on our mobile phones due to me going underground in the parking garage -- not wanting our conversation to end.

As soon as I'd get out of the car and into the elevator, I'd call my momma back and resume our conversation until I reached my floor by elevator; we loved staying in close contact with one another. Something was soothing about hearing her voice every single day.

When I finally reached my office, I'd log onto my computer and review my work activities for the day. Afterward, I'd send my momma an email, Subject line: 'Checking In!' Sometimes my mom would beat me to it and send her morning email first.

This was a daily ritual that we shared.

Several years ago, my mom's life was turned upside down, her sense of stability shaken to the core. Losing a job can do that to you.

After suffering this significant loss in her life, it took her over a year of diligently searching for gainful employment before she landed a new job. It wasn't her dream job, but it wasn't a complete nightmare either. She grew to appreciate the staff members that she supported and a few of the women she worked with. Still -- she longed for the job that she lost because so much of her identity was attached to her high profile position at a multi-million dollar complex in the heart of the inner city. She helped to establish the office and was the trusted and respected go-to for many-many years. She was completely committed to her job and the community and was loved and respected by all who had come to know her.

At her new job, she didn't care for her lunch hour, because she often ate alone. This wasn't an intentional exclusion; it's just that the other women ate as a group at an hour earlier. My mom still felt "some kind of way" because this was quite an adjustment for her. She was accustomed to being the glue that held things together and certainly included in everything - especially lunch!

While I don't love my job, I don't hate it either. Simply put, it's not aligned with my destiny. Many people find themselves in this situation and they manage, just like I am managing. My mom's job was not aligned with her destiny either (she'd much rather work in a role that allowed her to use the very best of her skills, abilities, and talents). In both cases, our jobs paid the bills, and our shared dreams for something better was the basis of our desire to support, encourage and uplift each other every day before going to work.

Having each other to lean on daily was instrumental to our ability to cope, as was the case when I was a child. It was just I and she for the larger part of our lives.

PARTS OF OUR LIVES

We were a small family of 5 people on my maternal side.

A married couple adopted my mom at the age of three. My mom shared stories of a hellish childhood in her adoptive home. She was a strong and courageous little girl who grew to be a strong and courageous woman.

By the time my mom was 17, her adoptive parents died my mom told me that anything of value left to her was stolen and mishandled by known adults. My mom was left alone and abandoned in a dilapidated apartment building, struggling to navigate a rather cold world and forced into adulthood sooner than later.

This was my mom's sad welcome to adulthood.

In spite of this, my mom made away.

I watched my mom over the years struggle to maintain some resemblance of a family with existing family members. Mostly, I never liked what I heard or saw; I always felt that she should never have to beg anyone for his or her love and acceptance. However, she did so and often felt hurt. I'll never forget her pain.

I never established a relationship much more than an occasional friendship with relatives on my mom's side – and those relationships fizzled out to non-relationships. So, essentially, my mom was my only maternal family member, period.

My mom longed for a sense of family no matter the cost. And it's a normal feeling to want to feel loved, accepted, needed, wanted and appreciated by a core group of people called family.

Now, about me – I'm her only child. She always wanted to have more children and embarked on twice failed adoptions to make that happen. This left my mother feeling inadequate, empty and broken-hearted. My mother could no longer bear children, so options like adoption seemed like a viable solution; my stepfather always wanted a child, which my mother was unable to produce. This was hard on their marriage.

My mother loved me with every fiber of her being. I loved and worshipped the ground that My Miss Bee walked on.

As a young mother, at only 21 with two kids, I worked my way up from government support to a high ranking federal position and CEO of FlightsInStilettos®, LLC.

You'd never known I had received government assistance for food and housing. I mastered the ability to make everyone think I was eating steak for dinner when I was eating hot dogs. My children were well dressed and well mannered and so was I.

Before my marriage to JM, I raised my two children as a single parent. I remember one time someone told me that I would be a "broke down baby mama" if I continued my pregnancy with my second child. However, quite the opposite happened. You see, I was covered by all those prayers my momma had been praying over me and for the welfare and protection of my children, her grandchildren.

In 2017, I married my longtime companion, JM. We had a dream wedding. Her nor I ever thought such a thing would happen to either of us but it did. My mom was deeply conflicted about my choice to marry JM because of her deep Christian values. I understood how she felt; I used to be brainwashed like that too until I met JM. I would always tell my mother that adults have the right to live their lives according to their convictions and everyone has to be responsible for their salvation.

My mom pictured me marrying a tall, handsome, educated and financially stable man who would cut her grass, change her car oil and take out her trash.

Instead, I married a tall, attractive, successful woman who loved me fully and completely, who could afford to pay someone to cut my mom's grass, change her car oil and take out her trash. JM's family owns one of the largest black-owned businesses in the city – those hot dog dinners eventually turned into steak and lobster dinners.

Over time, my mom's love for me prevailed, and she grew to love JM just as much, becoming quite the proud mother-in-law. JM was now an extension of her super small family; she took care of my mom and was there for my mom in every way possible. My mom also witnessed how much

Julie cared for my two children and me, and my mom felt I landed in safe and protective arms. She exhaled.

Sure, I have family on my paternal side, which I only see around holidays or at special events. They are a very close-knit family, but I'm not in the clique.

I loved my paternal grandmother and I can still hear her calling my name, 'PEEEEEAAACHHHHESSSS!'. My childhood nickname was Peaches. Every time I'd visit my grandma, I'd put money in her hands and she loved that. I wanted my grandma to get her favorite Chinese food - Pork Yak, all she wanted. I used to call my grandmother "Eyewitness News" because you could call my grandma to find out just about anything on anyone in the family. LOL, She never had a problem spilling the beans.

After a long bout of sickness, she passed away surrounded by her family, leaving a hole in the hearts of her 13 kids and tons of offspring. I miss my grandma tremendously.

The paternal side of my family always maintained a cordial and accepting relationship with my mom and still considered her their favorite sister-in-law. They always told her she was.

My father and mother had been divorced for most of my life, but this didn't matter – they still accepted her and welcomed her into their lives. It was common for them to invite my mom and his other children's mothers, to their functions – because they accepted everyone.

My mom spoke fondly of her first love, my father. She admitted it. My dad possessed qualities my mom loved such as being a hard worker (she spoke of him at one point being the only working man in his household with over 6 or more adult siblings living in a cramped 3 bedroom house in the projects, with her. My mom stayed with my dad in the projects with all of his siblings because her teenage pregnancy was a disgrace to her adoptive parents.

He'd bring her home Burger King sandwiches after his long shifts at Burger King, smelling of French fry grease. Sometimes this would be her only meal, which played a part in me being a smaller than average baby). After I was born, for a few years I lived with my grandma and my aunts. I can recall my aunts taking good care of me, cornrowing my hair. My mom hated my hair like that – she wanted my hair in long ponytails with ribbons.

She also considered him a smart man – acing his GED on the first try. Nevertheless, she also learned that he had ways he would not change - which ultimately suffocated and killed their marriage.

My mom eventually put on her "big girl" panties and left, after which divorce was granted. I always felt that my dad loved us, but he sure had a funny way of showing it.

She later married Small Johnson.

As it turned out, Mr. Johnson was a hardworking man; he stepped up to the plate and was responsible for potty training me (in earlier years) and once they got married, he took care of the household, but not my mother. He was anal about shit that didn't matter and I hated riding in the car with him because he'd always say the *"driver needs to be comfortable"* – that meant shit had to go his way with the music and car temperature.

As a young girl, I was introduced to multi-level marketing and get rich quick shit by Mr. Johnson that often left us broke.

His entire family treated me like their own. His mother and sisters adored me, and I loved them. His mother often asked my mom to let me come stay in the country with her, and I do mean country. I went down there for years and there was no plumbing system in the bathroom. I used a bucket for the toilet. My mom had to dump the bucket down the back of the hill, behind the trailer. I remember my aunts (by marriage) bathing me in the living room in a basin that needed to be filled with warm water.

That was the life I knew and I loved it. I'd play "up road" as they'd call playing up the street with the other family members. I played with the dog, Rex that was chained to the side of the house but was a beloved pet. This family-owned a significant amount of land – like a compound and many of the siblings built their own homes with their own hands and lived in this rural community where I loved spending time. I had a good time in the country eating my Grandma Blanche's famous potato salad. She loved me and I felt it. Grandma Blanche's passing was particularly hard on my mom because she loved her like a mother.

After several years of a flat lined fledgling marriage, my mom and I were abandoned.

My mom was a stay at home mom. So, when we were abandoned, this threw us into instant poverty and imminent homelessness.

On the day when this happened, I was in my late teens – a typical teenager; I had, once again, stayed out all night, nowhere to be found with my older man-friend. When I met this man-friend, I was only 16 but told him I was 18. I did the whole "meet the parents' things" and that's when my real age was revealed. He didn't seem to care, but it now made sense to him why I didn't know how to drive, didn't have a job and had "strict" parents. He eventually taught me how to drive and gave me my first car. Fatherly shit.

I'd often stay out all night against my parents' rules after meeting my man-friend; occasionally, when I'd come back home, my mom would leave a note on the door that said: *"Go back to where you came from"*. At that moment, I was sort of happy – you know, a whipped love-struck dumb teenager. However, when I saw the look on my man-friend's face that said "You ain't got to go home, but you got to get the hell out of my car" – I knew I'd better make it right with my mom and step-dad, or a chic was going to be sleeping in the back yard.

When I finally made it home and realized we had been abandoned, my man-friend who had shown some signs of being controlling was the only savior I had. With my sense of security and stability shaken, he was the only person I could rely on for the basics such as food, clothing and transportation. Mom had no income when we were left abandoned. We'd soon be homeless if we couldn't find someplace else affordable to live.

This created an unhealthy situation and dependency on man-friend – but I now needed him and the control was just part of what I had to deal with to make it and to help my mom financially.

When I was 17, my mom, left broke and desperate put any last ounce of dignity and pride that she had left to the side and filed for child support. She had no choice; we needed the money. My dad was pissed, but shit, it was time for him to pay up.

We ended up barely getting by after my mom found a rent-controlled apartment and a new job as a nanny. When I was younger my mom worked as a nanny and was a damn good one and had impeccable references. She knew that she could always return to that kind of work to support us, like she used to. When I was a little girl.

My man-friend was my only source of income.

In my late teens through my early 20's I was physically and emotionally abused and this abuse was exacerbated by lack of a male presence in my life.

I had never had a black eye before -- but I had finally experienced what that kind of blow was like. Yeah, I saw motherfucking stars like the cartoon characters when I was hit with that blow to the eye. I remember the abuser pulling all of the telephone cords out of the wall so that I couldn't call for help. Eventually, I was able to leave his house and I remember a group of men that pulled up next to me in their car as I was driving home – staring at my black eye. Again, I never had a black eye and didn't know what to do about it – but just let it be black, then blue and swollen.

I remember trying to hide my eye from my mom, but I couldn't and when she saw me, she just cried and cried. I wanted her to beat the abuser's ass – but she was no match for him.

There was no one to protect me.

After a day or two, my eye was still black; I snuck out to a payphone to call my abuser. I knew it was wrong, but I wanted to hear his voice to see if he was still so very sorry. I felt sorry that he was "so sorry" and went back to him, thinking that maybe it was just a horrible mistake that would never happen again. While I had this black eye, I went back to him and I can recall riding out to a basketball court with him and his friends; I still had the black eye.

Everyone knew how it happened and tried to avoid eye contact. I remember walking into the gym, and the one person that made eye contact with me was this white man, who looked at me and shook his head as if he felt sorry for me. At the moment, I felt ashamed and embarrassed but I didn't have the strength to leave. I was scared too – thinking how would I take care of myself and help my mom if I didn't have man-friend? But I also remember having that black eye and smiling at man-friend.

I became obsessed with catching man-friend with other women. Because he was my sole caretaker, he provided me with my car, and I had access to several other luxury vehicles and cash. He didn't pay too much attention to my spending because he was generous to me. What he didn't give me, I'd just take. Spending sprees up Georgetown was common. Hell, I was dressed cute…. that was the one thing going right.

At one point, I was caught up in a terrible love triangle with man-friend. It drove me insane. I would use my car to perform stakeouts to catch him cheating; if I wasn't staking out, I was stalking. I went many nights driving around in the early morning hours just to catch him cheating. Often, I did, and I would terrorize the object of his affection.

My obsession was so bad that my friends stopped hanging out with me. I was the only person in my group of friends who had a car and spare cash. However, if you were going to ride with me, we first had to track down man-friend. If I was satisfied with his whereabouts then we could go on and have fun. If I wasn't, my friends had to wait in the car and watch me engage in contemptuous battles with man-friend that lasted for hours. Sometimes, they'd say, "fuck it" and leave me and catch the bus back home.

One time I was in my car when I caught him cheating; I jumped out of the car while it was moving, just to launch at and attack the other woman. From that point forward man-friend labeled me "crazy". I didn't even know I had that side to my personality.

After the numerous stakeouts and stalking, he took my car away from me and said he was taking my car because that wasn't why he gave it to me.

Not having a car was no problem. By then I had new girlfriends with cars.

I can recall a time when I was hunting him down and called one of his side chicks. I called her home in the wee hours of the morning like I was that bitch (even though she was sleeping with my man-friend) and she answered the phone. I said, let me speak to "man-friend". She said: *"Maybe he's here and maybe he isn't"* and hung up the phone.

I no longer had transportation. That sent a rage through my blood vessels and bones that I will never forget. I foamed at the mouth in anger with revenge on my mind. I paced back and forth thinking about how I could make my way to where they were. I was going to have the last "say", not her.

I did the only reasonable thing to do at 5 am. I looked on wmata.com and found out how to catch subway trains and buses from my home to about 40 miles away in another state. The entire way, I remained focused on fucking up man-friend, his car, and her car. I also kept in mind what if he wasn't there.

I made it to the next state in rush hour in optimal time. Public transportation was on point that day. I didn't know where this chic lived, but I knew the general vicinity. I had sharpened my investigative skills over the years, so I was on the hunt for their cars in the parking lot. This was a big motherfucking complex -- mixed with townhouses and apartments. I had a lot of ground to cover on foot but didn't care; that bitch got smart with me and she was going to pay.

Man-friend was smart; he parked his car in another community. I spotted it, but I didn't see her car, the one he bought her. So that was the fake-out.

I kept walking through the apartment complex, getting angrier by the minute. It was cold too. Then finally, I spot her piece of shit car *(I did my best to etch the word "fuck you hoe" on the side of her car)*. But damn, what building did she live in? I didn't give a fuck. I started at the top of each building, going door by door and worked my way down to the bottom floor and until I struck gold. Knock. Knock, Knock.

I knocked on the door (feeling justified with every knock) and she answered the door. I smirked at her while she had a look of bewilderment, like *I know this bitch didn't just catch the bus....* see she thought she was safe, talking that shit because I didn't have a car.

He came to the door; I reached out toward his face, closed my eyes and scratched like a wild untamed cat drawing blood. They were both rather concerned not knowing what my next move would be. If I was crazy enough to take a three-hour bus and train ride, plus a 30-minute walk through an unknown neighbor all before 8 am in another state – who knows what else I'd do?

Man-friend gathered his things and said, "Come on, I'm taking you home." I looked at the other woman, smirked and said, "I told you he'd leave with me." I thought I did something special. Like I had won a grand fucking prize.

Ultimately, man-friend had convinced me that the only way he'd be happy is if we all lived together. Like -- some sister-wives type shit. For a minute, I considered it, pondering that we'd live in a nice townhouse and she'd work, while I hung out with him all day…. why not? I'd have the best of man-friend all day. Fucking all day. He'd be too tired to pay her any real attention.

Well, I came to my senses and it never happened. Hell no, that shit was never going to work. I could see the headline news story now: *"Double homicide and suicide"*.

However, this was the kind of life I was subjected to and this was my sad and sorry introduction to love and relationships.

Man-friend fought to keep me, but in the end, I detached and he let me go so that I could be loved and happy. During one final last fight, he realized something wonderfully different happened to me and changed me and thus he no longer had a grip on me.

After a few other failed relationships after main-friend, I had given up on love and focused on raising my children.

Then one night, I got the strength to go to a friend's milestone birthday party and there I met the love of my life.

I met my JM, who truly was the **princess** in shining armor who rescued me.

I didn't even know I was worthy of being loved until I met her. I didn't know I was worthy of having a normal home life until I settled with her. I didn't know I was worthy of having her all to myself until she showed me I was. I didn't know I was worthy of the finer things in life until she showed me that I was. I was so accustomed to being lied to, rejected, abused, neglected and made to feel second best, that I had a hard time adjusting to being shown love and tenderness. When she did something nice for me, I thought I had to do something 10x more to earn that kind of treatment.

She showed me that I just needed to be myself and that I was indeed worthy. I was so accustomed to being cheating on that I looked for it for her, but never found anything.

I too rescued her. I fought fiercely to have her all to myself; I felt something very safe and comforting with her and from her, and I could not ever again let anyone love another person more than me. Especially not JM.

We found something solid and true within each other. We both exhaled.

My mom, feeling desperate, abandoned, unloved and ashamed, turned to the only person she could rely on - God.

These acts of betrayal by the men in my mom's life not only hurt my mom; they etched in my mind that men are never to be trusted, especially after experiencing it personally with man-friend.

My biological dad remarried and I was not included in that phase of his life. I endured this rejection as a little girl well into my adulthood. I can recall my phone number being blocked so that I could not call their home to speak to my father. As a result of these actions, I experienced a very severe form of rejection that I never got over. This was the first heartbreak I experienced from a man that set the tone for future heartbreaks from men.

So, from an early age, I learned that some men abandon you and break your heart and are not to be trusted. Later I learned that some men would abuse you.

While my mom was bruised, she was never broken and I have always admired her strength in the face of adversity. She truly outwardly showed love, but I always knew her heart was forever broken, irreparably damaged. However, she poured her entire life into God, me, my kids, chasing a fledgling relationship with her family member and her church families. She enjoyed her church family and the bonds created.

Through all of this shared pain, my mom and I grew incredibly close. I had her and she had me. I loved her with all of my heart. I always wished I could take her pain away, but I could not. Instead, I was experiencing that same sense of pain and abandonment that visited her since birth.

In my mom's younger years, she discovered she had amazing talent, the gift of singing. She could sing....let me rephrase that, she could "sanggggg".

She experienced so much pain and heartbreak throughout her life that she learned to express herself through song and writing. She was both a well-respected gospel singer and playwright.

Being an adopted child, my mom always felt a sense of abandonment. I can only imagine the pain of growing up feeling unwanted and then suffering at the hands of her adoptive parents, then suffering at the hands of men.

I despised men as husbands and caregivers, but not as human beings and friends. I never wanted them close to me.

Now, going back to the daily routine with my mom, at 5:45 pm, she would call me when she got in the car on her way home from work -- she'd call me and say, "Peaches, you in the car?" LOL. It was hysterical because she knew good and well I was in the car. Some days if I was cranky, I would get irritated with that question. Sometimes I would call her first, but she wouldn't answer if she was already on a call and I can recall acting like a spoiled brat and calling her repeatedly until she dropped the other call for me.

If that wasn't enough, my mom actively used both Facebook and Instagram. So, in the evenings, we would exchange comments via social media. When I say that my mom and I were incredibly close and in constant communication, it's the absolute truth. My spouse, JM, took a back seat to the communication I shared with my mom. She was okay with this because she enjoyed watching the closeness I shared with my mom.

I needed to hear her voice and feel her unconditional love and support - every day. And because we spoke each day, I saw her only several times a month. Her love for me was consuming and so fulfilling. I yearned to speak to my mom all the time because it felt so good to do so.

During the summer of 2018, our lives and super small family were about to increase. My daughter announced her pregnancy with her longtime boyfriend.

I had mixed feelings outwardly, but secretly, my mom and I were ecstatic and had already started planning on how we would divide our time with our new bundle of joy. We would send each other pictures found on the Internet of what we thought the baby would look like. We knew the baby would be a caramel color and would certainly have black curly hair like the father since he's part Sri Lankan.

The upcoming birth of this baby meant everything to her, to us both. I felt ready to be a grandma.

This baby would be an extension of my mom's bloodline. We all wanted this baby and felt that this new life was a true gift from God.

We found out later in the summer of 2018 that my daughter was having a baby boy.

A few weeks later, my mom and I starting planning my daughter's baby shower. My mom was going to oversee the games, and me and JM -- well, everything else.

My God, my mom was so excited about her first great-grandson, and nicknamed him "Binky". From that point forward, we all called him Binky.

During this same time, my mom was also complaining almost daily about her bowels and severe stomach pain that would not go away; I was worried, but I knew that whatever it was, my mom was on top of it. My mom was super in tuned with her body and researched every single ailment, medicine and out of the ordinary symptoms. I'd always call my mom before calling the doctor -- because she knew just as much. I believed in my heart, like every other time she felt sick- that this too would pass.

Following My Inner Voice

For some strange reason, at the beginning of 2018, I felt an overwhelming urge to spend more time with my mom. There was a constant powerful inner voice that I would hear encouraging me almost weekly. So we decided that we'd reserve every 4th Sunday for family day. She'd skip church and we'd gather the family together at my home for food and family fun. We all looked forward to the family day because that's primarily the only time my mom would see my eldest child, my son. She'd see my daughter more frequently because my daughter is very family-oriented. It was nothing for her to hop in her car and visit my mom on a whim. My son (although loving and caring) relied upon our designated family day, texting and calling my mom for his interactions with her.

Since I spoke to my mom multiple times every day, I didn't feel a sense of urgency to see her as frequently, until now. I felt a sense of urgency now more than ever; after all, she was getting older, was still unmarried and did everything on her own as a single woman. She always enjoyed being in our company and playing our favorite game Pit. She used to laugh her ass off playing that game Pit!

I was waiting for a magical age before telling her to give up her job and just move in with us. There was a part of me that didn't want her to give up on finding love again, and possibly remarrying, so I was okay with her living on her own under our watchful eye.

I enjoyed our moments together immensely and hated to see my mom leave after spending time with her. I felt sadness in my heart and a sinking feeling whenever I had to say bye to my mom. I would always try to get her to spend the night and she would always say she couldn't without her C-PAP machine. So, JM and I would walk her to her car, put gas and lunch money in her hands and watch her drive off until we could no longer see her taillights. I anxiously awaited her call or texts letting me know she had made it home safely.

In September 2018, my mom sent me an e-mail at work letting me know about her upcoming doctor's appointment on September 4, 2018. I heard that little voice inside that said: "Ask your mom if you could go with her to her doctor's appointment." So I did. My mom was so incredibly excited that I had asked; she eagerly looked forward to my support and my being there with her. I was also secretly excited because this was out of the norm and I could see my momma's sweet little face on a random Tuesday. She's my 60-year-old mom, so no matter my age, time, space or distance, I longed for her love, affection, and attention, which she so freely gave. I knew that I was the center of her joy and I loved it. My mother adored me. Here's a text that she sent to me in 2018 "I love you too precious!! You're my very heartbeat…You are more than I could have ever hoped for in a daughter. Just hearing your voice each day brings me life. Not quite sure what I did to deserve such a wonderful daughter, but God knew what he was doing when he gave you me. I've had a lot of wonderful things happen in my life, but hands down, God giving you me was the absolute best thing that could have ever happened to me. I'm so very proud of you, some days I look at you and can't believe you belong to me. Just blessed. ~Mom".

This is the kind of love I knew from only her. My entire life, I only felt the love from my mother, until I met JM.

I met my mom at her doctor's office one sunny day. She wasn't pleased with her visit, because she didn't feel she received adequate treatment. The directions she received during that visit didn't relieve her pain and only exacerbated her frustration.

After the doctor's office visit, I wasn't ready to leave my mom, so I asked her to have lunch at our favorite lunch spot. Every time we went to our favorite spot, we'd order the same meal - chicken fingers with honey mustard, 2 salmon Caesar salads and iced tea. She hipped me to that combination, LOL, but this time was different; my mom didn't eat. She couldn't because she needed to take her medicine on an empty stomach. She decided to sit and keep me company while I ate our favorite meal.

We laughed and talked about our favorite things; of course, the dominating topic would be my daughter's pregnancy and the plans for her baby shower in December 2018. Even after we talked about our favorite topics, we talked about them again, because she was in no hurry to return to her job 3 miles away, and I was in no hurry to leave my mother's company. I immensely enjoyed that moment with my momma.

This was the last meal I had with her.

BYE MOMMY

On October 6th, it was a brisk fall day and I was at home enjoying some quiet time with JM. We had just finished a delicious grilled lobster dinner and we were sipping on wine while enjoying a movie when suddenly my phone rang and it was my mom. She was in the hospital about not too far from my home. Her stomach wasn't feeling any better since her doctor's visit on Tuesday, so she decided to be seen in the emergency room.

JM and I dropped everything and went up to the hospital to see what was going on. When we arrived, my mom looked very much like her normal self, but I knew that she was dealing with something that was both quite serious for her and quite frightening.

JM and I stayed with my mom that night until every test result was received.

It was just as my mom knew; she was suffering from an intestinal blockage.

Once this was confirmed, my mom grew more and more frightened about what that meant for her life moving forward. She had just accepted a new job and was in transition since she had given her job her 2-week notice. She was perplexed with how to make the best possible decisions, because how in the world could she tell her new job that she could no longer start on the assigned start date and how would her medical bills be covered since she resigned from her current job, but would not have coverage on her new job for at least 60 days?

Nevertheless, we couldn't focus on any of that. In my mind, my mom would be just fine like all of the other times she checked herself in the emergency room and checked herself out.

Over the years, my mom made many visits to the ER, so to me, this was similar to one of those times.

On October 7, 2018, my mom was officially admitted to the hospital. My confidence was beginning to waver, because it appeared that my mom would be in the hospital a bit longer than usual with a condition a bit more serious than usual.

I still made jokes with her, telling her she could have the surgery and be the superwoman she was and report to work a week later; she no longer thought my optimism was funny, and I knew something wasn't right. I didn't want to believe that her condition was serious, although the signs were showing it was. It was hard to believe it because my mom was still talking and functioning and texting her friends and being her normal self – but she truly was not feeling well.

Once my mom was transferred to her new hospital room, I heard that inner voice again telling me to stay with her. Again, this inner voice was crystal clear and unmistakable. I never felt this undeniable yearning (that I could not ignore) to be by her side. I complied.

This was the one time I was glad I had the job I had and the kind of supervisor that I had who shared a close relationship with her mother. She was sympathetic to my yearning and duty to be by my mom's side.

For the next week, I was at the hospital from 8 am to about 8 pm daily. I didn't want to miss anything or anyone who had any influence over her healthcare. I took a trip to the mall to get my mom a better robe, slippers, a few house dresses, and even a new handbag… after all, if she's going to be there, she's going to look good.

While in the hospital, my ever so faithful and supportive mom wore her silk FlightsInStilettos® headscarf that she loved so much. That made me smile.

In the evenings, once I left the hospital, I would call my mom to check in on her. Remember, our ritual was to be in communication every day, by multiple forms – calls, texts, and social media.

I heard the inner voice again. This time it told me to post a message on Facebook expressing my disappointment in my mom's "friends" for not visiting her in the hospital. During her first week in the hospital, about 4 people visited her. I was appalled and outraged and posted a Facebook message to that effect.
She had been in the hospital for an entire week and the visits from "friends" were underwhelming. That broke my heart and still does when I think about it.

Other family members had made several visits during this time, sometimes coordinated when I wasn't there. Before my mom's hospitalization, I had not been in contact with her family members since early 2017.

By the second week and after my Facebook posts, as well as my mom's own communication with her friends, more of them and other associates visited her in the hospital. Even my biological dad's sisters visited my mom. Flowers were pouring in, calls and text messages increased exponentially.

Somehow during this time, both my mom's family member and I had put our guards down. We instinctively knew she was all we both had on some level and we had to work together to see my mom through. It was as if we had a good relationship and that we were on the same team…but that wasn't the case. That was the Holy Spirit taking over both of us because the petty shit had to take a back seat.

My children and spouse, JM, made multiple trips to the hospital and several of my mom's good friends sat with us during critical times at the hospital.

During one hospital visit, we captured my mom on video rubbing my daughter's stomach, connecting with her kicking great-grandson in the womb. That would be her last time connecting with her great-grandson.

My mom still appeared to be her normal self, but the condition of her intestines was anything but normal. The intestinal blockage was still there. There was a calm sense of urgency in the air. She had gone weeks unable to move her bowels or pass gas.

My mom's greatest fear was having surgery and being assigned a colostomy bag. This would surely impact her ability to start her new job, and in her mind, to hell with ever having a social life.

After several days of indecision on the part of the physicians regarding her care, I called a meeting with the medical staff to get concrete answers on what the plan was for her healthcare and getting my mom up an out of Holy Cross Hospital.

My mom's adoptive father died as a result of colon issues and was assigned a colostomy bag in the 60s. Times have changed and a colostomy bag in the 60s would not be the colostomy bag of 2018. Nevertheless, there was no convincing her that she wouldn't smell of human feces and everyone else wouldn't be able to smell it. She couldn't accept that and wanted a colostomy bag only as an absolute last option.

Momma was a trooper. She waited until the last possible moment to contact the Human Resources Officer of her new job to let them know of her hospitalization. Surprisingly, her new job was extremely diplomatic and reassured my mom that her job was safe. Whether true or not, I will always be grateful to whoever handled those communications with my mom. It would have been heartless to tell a woman already feeling low and sick that "Oh, yeah, good luck with your surgery, but we're not holding this job for you. Best of Luck!"

My mom felt an overwhelming sense of relief thinking she at least still had a job, and I did too – I felt this was a sign that things would be just fine. Surely they would be if the doctors could just get on the same page and get this thing over with. If only she could have the surgery, and a 4-week recovery at my house, she'd be back on her feet. We could finish planning the baby shower, then enjoy Thanksgiving, Christmas, the baby shower…life would go on as planned.

My mom's medical team eventually decided that surgery was the only option after non-surgical options did not produce the intended results.

The first surgery was 10 hours long. It was supposed to be 4 hours. She was taken to recovery and ultimately admitted to the Intensive Care Unit (ICU). When she awoke, she was in terrible pain, which was being managed. I was there every day with her, but something was amiss. Her vitals were fluctuating and she would monitor the machines and said she didn't feel right. The nurses would tell her to relax and that she should not monitor the machines. In my heart, I was skeptical because I knew my mom knew how to read the machines. My mom said, *"Peaches, something isn't right; if they take me to surgery again, I'm not going to make it."* By the 3rd day of this, we demanded that the surgeon take a look and see what the issue was. She was immediately prepped for a second surgery – the CT scans showed fluid in her belly area. She had fluid in the belly area because, during the initial surgery, they disconnected her bowels to remove the blockages and then reconnected her bowels. Unfortunately, this is a complication of this surgery.

The connection was compromised; for several days my mom's body was poisoned by her waste causing septic shock. This is especially dangerous in the abdominal area, which is in close proximity to all vital organs. She was experiencing the deadliest form of septic shock. Her body was going into shock and her organs began to shut down.

I can't put into words the feelings the came over me, but as she was in the holding area being prepped for her second emergency surgery to wash the compromised area. With tubes running in and out of her, I was an inconsolable wreck. My mom was icy cold to the touch. I screamed. I fell on the floor; I was holding her hand, crying hysterically. I did not care about anything other than what was happening to my mom. I fell out on the floor in pain and screamed in agony. I would pull myself together, run back in the surgical waiting area and look at my mom, who was weak and still looking at me while the oxygen mask was on her face. She was cold; I was confused; I was sad; I was scared.

JM and the nurses were telling me not to act like that, because it was stressing my mom. I couldn't help it, I could not control the fear I was experiencing. I saw the fear in her eyes.

I was whisked out of the pre-surgical area because of my hysteria. I panicked, and I screamed down the halls of the hospital then laid out on the floor.

This was the last time I saw my momma conscious.

I still believed I would see her again and we'd go home and plan the baby shower, Thanksgiving and Christmas. Except for this time, I was planning in my head how we would rearrange the furniture to move my mom in our home during her recovery.

My momma was taken back to ICU after the second surgery and was deemed "very sick". She was not conscious.

When I saw the condition that my mom was in, I abandoned all sense of reality and was a complete basket case with moments of sanity. I abandoned all sense of fashion; I had no idea if I had a wig on or just the stocking cap. I didn't care. My eyes were bloodshot red from crying and lack of sleep. I smelled my self…arms, musty from not bathing. Breath-funky from not eating or brushing my teeth.

While she was in the ICU, she was hooked to every life-sustaining machine available. I knew my mom looked bad and swollen, but the healthcare professionals kept giving me hope, so I thought everything was still going to be just fine. Even her church friends were giving me hope. But in reality she was dying.

She had one nurse solely devoted to her care during the various shifts. At this point, I stopped caring for myself. I could not leave her side. On two occasions at night, they had to use the machines to shock her heart. When that happened, they made me leave the room and I walked out, looking back and crying, looking forward, then looking back at my mommy. I'd take a few steps again, look back at my mommy and cry... I felt helpless. Even still, I thought that after that, my mommy was going to be okay. I had swollen bright eyes because I knew they worked on my mommy and no one said she died...so there was still hope.

I was standing in the hallway alone and one nurse came to me to comfort me. I will never forget the nurse that cared for her those days and nights, but it's the night shift nurse who I will never ever forget. She was a black woman with a very strong stature with very short hair. I remember speaking to her because I felt that if I treated the nurses with love, they would save my mommy.

My mom was hooked to several machines with several kinds of medicines pumping in and out to sustain what was left of her. This special nurse was like an ultimate chemist. She knew when to increase liquid drips when to pull back, when to turn it off, when to turn it on. This nurse wasn't just "doing her job"; this nurse was working to save my momma's life. She told me she was. I believed her.

The hospital staff shared with me that my mom was the sweetest patient they had ever worked with. Because of her being this ray of light, they worked at unprecedented levels to save her life. They exceeded doses of medicine to see if she had a fighting chance. They were committed to helping this angel on an unprecedented level not normally experienced by most patients. I saw it with my own eyes. I saw that special nurse bust her ass for my mom.

One night, I desperately tried to get the special nurse to break protocol and tell me if my mother was going to live or die. Up until that point, they were doing what they were trained to do – give me hope. I took that hope. It was my hope. The special nurse looked at me, I looked at her and a tear rolled down her face. Then a tear rolled down my face. I knew that it was going to take more than hope to save my mom.

That was the last time I saw the special nurse.

Because I wasn't in my right state of mind and denial, I still believed that although my mom looked in a manner I had never on earth seen her (swollen beyond recognition and cold to the touch), that all of that was going to be reversed, because I convinced myself that she was getting better because the machines still showed heart activity.

On October 21, 2018, the unthinkable happened. The ICU doctor asked me to gather the family together for a meeting. I was informed that they had done all they could do for my mom and I needed to decide to keep her on life support or to make her comfortable, which is code for take her off the machines and let her expire naturally.

When this happened, family and clergy, as well as members of her church were present. I am her only living blood relative, so all of the decisions rested with me.

Her clergy convinced me that a miracle could happen, and science said otherwise. I made eye contact with everyone in the room. It was the most painful and agonizing decision I would ever make. "Make my mommy comfortable," I said. I believed that a miracle was possible.

On that same day, October 21, 2018, the ICU doctor made my mom comfortable by slowly removing all the life-sustaining equipment – making sure to inject her with pain medication, although she was not expected to feel any pain.

I sat at my mother's head. I rubbed her forehead. I held her cold hands. I whispered in her ear repeatedly *"I am here mommy and I love you mommy".*

My mother peacefully slipped into eternal rest surrounded by over 20 friends and family members.

In momma's final moments in the ICU, I was seated by her side and laid on her shoulder, I kissed her forehead and her hands; I rubbed her forehead and her hair, I held her hands, rubbed her feet and repeatedly let her know I was there and she was loved as she transitioned. Her Goddaughter played gospel music for her. I saw light tears stream down past her temples as she took her last breath.

I'll never know what final things she heard, but I pray that my final words to her, that I am here, and I love you, were what she heard. I pray that the last thing she ever felt was my everlasting love.

Her room was filled with music, love, and light as she took her last breath.

It was a moment in time that I will never forget. I will never get over it. I will never get past it. I will never be normal again.

It was the most peaceful moment and yet the most gut-wrenching moment at the same time.

Because my mom was single and never remarried, I was always concerned about her safety.

Oddly, I felt some peace knowing she did not die alone, beat and raped and thrown in a gutter.

I saw my mother, my protector, my best friend, my confidant, my motivator, my heart, my daily chat buddy, my Miss Bee, my entire everything leave this earth and walk into the light safely into God's arms. She was in complete and perfect peace and left all the joys, pain, financial struggles and unrequited love and loyalty of life on earth, behind.

She left me behind too; however, I understand her new spiritual mission and that she's here with me more than ever.

REFLECTING BACK

Thinking back to the day that started as an ordinary day on **September 21, 2018**, it was anything but ordinary.... it was the beginning of the last 30 days I'd ever spend with my mother in this lifetime. I never expected her to die.

Let that sink in.

We were living in my mom's final 30 days and did not know it. That's why my inner voice was louder than usual.

That's why I felt a sense of urgency to spend time with my mother in 2018.

That's why it was important for me to go to the doctor's office with my mother for the **last time.**

That's why I felt the urge to have lunch at our favorite lunch spot with my mother for the **last time.**

That's why without hesitation, I dropped everything and didn't give a damn about my job so that I could spend every moment around the clock with her at the hospital for the **last time.**

That's why I felt an urge to appeal to her friends on Facebook to visit my mom in the hospital because it would be their **last time.**

We all were living, loving, reveling, planning, visiting, hugging, socializing, singing, laughing, kissing, holding and praying with my mom in her last 30 days of life on this earth.

None of us knows when that 30-day countdown will begin for our lives or the lives of people we love, but it is important to understand, hear and follow your inner voice.

Think back to a time when your loved one passed away and count back 30-days. How did you spend those last 30 days with your loved one?

Moving forward, make every **single day** count because you never know when that countdown will begin on your life or the ones you love.

As I wade through the rivers of inconsolable pain, as I learn to exist in this new normal and as I strive to complete incomplete missions in my mother's honor, I ask you to listen to your inner voice.

Your inner voice will guide you down the appropriate life's path. Listen to it.

Looking back at the 30 days of **September 21 - October 21, 2018**, I have no regrets, because I was obedient to my inner voice. I spent an unprecedented amount of time sitting at my mother's side loving her, supporting her, assuring her, talking to her, consoling her, rubbing her face, at times laughing and crying with her, listening to her, praying over her and letting her know that from those moments forward, I would never leave her side and I would always love her.

LOVE IN A BOX

You don't realize how permanent death is until you lose someone whom you love with all of your heart. The deeper the love, the deeper the grief. People always say, "You'll see your loved one again" – please understand, the loved one you knew on earth in earthly form, you will never see again. My mom is now a spirit, and as much as I want to wallow in my grief, despair, heartbreak, agony, and pain – I must channel that energy because my mom cannot connect with that vibration. Her spirit does not exist in a place that can experience hurt, pain, agony, and despair.

I am constantly acutely aware of my vibration and always aspire to vibrate high so that the flow of love, energy, and light from my mom's spirit to me remains unblocked.

When we lose a parent, the greatest thing we fear is the loss of their love. In time, you will come to know your beloved departed in a new way; you will once again feel their love as if they are sitting in another room. But it will take time.

Someone once asked me how does it feel to lose your mom? All that I could think of is that I no longer have to worry about facing or anticipating that kind of pain again because I already had as an only child of a single parent. It is the most unimaginable pain that you will ever experience as a human being.

As I think about how I survived the trauma I experienced as a result of the unexpected loss of my mother, I can recall the first night leaving the hospital after she passed away. The emotional pain was so unbearable and intense that I would stiffen my body like a wooden board and tense every muscle in my body, clench my fists and throw my head back and scream and cry in agony. I went in and out of reality denying that she had passed away. This continued for weeks.

During the day I would sit in a room with my mother's picture, the last clothes she had on and even her wig. I had my mother's pair of shoes last worn and I'd put those on and walk around the house. This scared JM and she made me stop. I'd Google search "where is my mommy?" I wanted my mother back.

My mind kept telling me that my mom shouldn't be alone and that I should be with her. I kept telling myself that she'd want me to kill myself and be with her.

Please understand, my mom was adopted, she has no known blood relatives. She was all that I knew and all that I had on my maternal side. There is not a trace of her left. Not a brother who looks like her, or a cousin who sings like her, or a grandmother who cooks like her. My entire matriarch is gone. All I have now are memories of my Miss Bee.

JM thought the pain of losing my mom would burst my heart wide open. I wanted to die. What the fuck else did I have to live for?

I didn't want to pick up and carry on in this life without My Miss Bee.

For the first three months, I was suicidal and because this was something I was actively planning to do by (getting my insurance papers in order, writing my resignation for my job) JM had to take off from work to monitor me to keep me from killing myself. When JM did return to work she worried herself sick every morning before she left for work whether or not she'd come home from work and find me hanging in my closet. She would call me every 30 minutes to make sure that I was still alive.

The primary reason I survived this was because of the dedication, love, and support from my spouse JM. I could not and I ***would not*** have been able to make it without her. Her love for me and her desire for me to make it is the reason why I made it. Initially, I did not possess the will to make it. I was solely making it because of the love I had for JM and my children.

It's funny because my mom used to always say to me *"I'm glad that you have JM"*. She knew how much of a force JM was in my life and that our partnership made me strong.

Allow your spouse and loved ones to love and support you through your pain.

JM's constant support and the reminder that I still have people here who need me and her encouragement that I should continue living for them was crucial to my recovery.

She would say to me *"Aren't we enough for you to fight for and keep living?"*

I would also think about the high degree of pain losing my mother caused me, and how I would not want to bring that pain on my two children. JM and I are all they have. If they lost me, they'd only have JM. JM can't make it without me. So, I had to find a better way to cope with my pain and grief.

I went under intensive therapy and the care of a psychiatrist. Both of these interventions helped me tremendously coupled with the support of my spouse and children.

Seek therapy. Don't be ashamed.

A month after my mom passed away I tried to return to work. The first time I went to the office, I cried as soon as I sat at my desk, and immediately ran out of the office to my car and drove back home. I wasn't ready to return to work life for months.

Take the appropriate time off from work to deal with your grief.

Some people throw themselves into work - everyone is different. I needed to disconnect completely from work responsibilities and get my head straight so that I could focus when I returned to work.

I needed a way to stay connected with my mom and to honor her legacy. Because she didn't have any blood relatives other than me, I was scared that no one would remember my mom except me. I immediately sought out ways to preserve her memory and to keep her memory alive in the hearts of people who want to remember her.

My mom always wanted to be a published author, I'm writing this book to complete a mission that was uncompleted by her – in her honor.

Keep your loved one's legacy alive in ways that they would have loved. Complete actions in your power that your loved one did not.

My mom was a humble woman and didn't place value on material things. My mom was an avid reader and a collector of books. She amassed a prize collection of books.

I had the painstakingly difficult task of going through my mom's belongings; I kept everything that I knew that she valued. The smaller items I kept and put them in a beautiful locked box, which I refer to as ***Love in a Box***. Everything about my mom that I love that I can look at and smile at and remember her by is now all *love in a box*. The 43 years worth of my best memories shared with my mommy are now ***Love in a Box***.

Keep your loved one's treasures in a special place. Make it your special place. Love in a Box.

I used to fear death, but not anymore. I know that when it's my time, my mom's spirit will be waiting for me and we will be reunited again. I have accepted the fact that I have to keep living because my mom would never want me to leave my children and Julie behind. If anything my mom is probably enjoying her new spiritual assignment and is now in the best position than ever to watch over our entire family.

Once you accept what has happened, you will be able to think more clearly about how to live the rest of your life without your deceased loved one in your life. Find your reasons to keep living.

I had to learn to slowly find joy in the simple things again. For months, no matter how sunny it was outside, all I saw was darkness. I had to learn how to live again and not just exist. It ultimately was a choice I had to make. I could live out the rest of my days depressed and in agony or I could live out the rest of my days loving my remaining family and creating the best possible memories for them (because when you die that's all that's left). I chose to live. I chose to accept that my family here loves me and they are worthy of my love and life. I was energized thinking of how I could keep my mom's legacy alive; that's what she'd expect out of the strong independent daughter she raised.

Keep living and cherish the memories of your loved one. Think of something every day that makes you smile and remember why you loved your departed loved one.

In the summer of 2019, I heard my inner voice again. It told me to go to a specific store in a specific neighborhood. I rarely run errands in the evenings after work, but the inner voice was loud and clear. So I went to a specific store. After browsing around for a little while, I happened to look in the Women's section; my eyes opened wide and my heart started beating super-fast. In the aisle of the store, I saw the special nurse in ICU who I saw with my own eyes working her ass off to save my mom. At that moment, I knew that's why I was led to this specific store at this specific time. I thought to myself, should I say something? Before I could complete the thought, my legs and cart were already moving in her direction. My heart started beating faster. I left my cart in the middle of the store, purchases be damned and walked toward the special nurse.

I said, *"Do you remember me?"* Her eyes were also now glossy and wide. She said, "Of course I remember you; I will never forget you or your mom. I have worked with many patients, but your mom is the one that will forever stand out. Your mom was the absolute sweetest person and I want you to know that the entire ICU loved your mom and we put our all into saving your mom."

It was extremely cathartic for me to experience that because I always wondered what happened to the special nurse.

After my mom's funeral, I sent the special nurse my mom's program from her funeral. It was important for me to share with her who my mom was, what she looked like and what she meant to others. The special nurse said that she knew my mom was special because of the steady stream of visitors to the ICU (after my Facebook post appeal).

She shared with me that the ICU nurses called her when my mom passed away and she told me that she was at the gym and fell to her knees in the parking lot in grief and pain.

In the store, her eyes filled with tears. Whenever someone cries for my mom, strength comes over me and I comfort them. I then shed tears once out of their sight.

She and I embraced for what seemed like a minute in the middle of the store, my heart pounding and my mind remembering that she spent time caring for my momma in her final moments. I have been on a mission to connect with her caregivers who were closest to her during her final moments, searching for any words she may have whispered to them. My momma spoke of her love for her family, and everyone in the ICU knew about her soon-to-be-born great-grandson.

The special nurse and I knew that this chance encounter was meant to be because she was moving to CA in two weeks.

Divinely, I believe wholeheartedly that the chance meeting was orchestrated on a divine level to bring peace and closure on some level to the special nurse and me.

In February 2019, my daughter finally gave birth to my first grandson and my mom's first great-grandson, baby KBT. His birth seemed almost ordained by God after the sudden passing of my mother. Ironically, everyone who knew my mom says that without a doubt, KBT bears a resemblance to my mom. From the moment he was born, we made a promise to keep her memory alive by ensuring that baby KBT is educated about her legacy.

Every time I look at KBT, every time I hold KBT, I feel that I am embracing a living part of my mom that exists through his existence. This was yet another reason I had to keep living.

My very small family still meets every 4th Sunday for food, fun, laughter and to remember my momma. Sometimes we get together more than that. It's even more important to us now than ever, to spend time together loving each other, as we all raise our newest family member, Baby KBT.

I've still have never seen my step-dad.

My biological dad has tried to make amends for the lost time over the years. I have accepted his attempts.

I have not been in communication with anyone on my mom's side since her funeral.

Unfortunately, my mom passed away before ever seeing her encouragement come into fruition -- celebrities, wearing FlightsInStilettos®. She would have been immensely proud and happy about my accomplishments.

I know that she would have printed out the pictures of every celebrity spotted wearing FlightsInStilettos® and put the pictures in her living room, with that proud mama smile on her face.

I miss my mother so much every single day. I look forward to going to sleep every night hoping that I can dream about her.

I'm adjusting now to my new normal thanks to the unwavering love and support of my beloved spouse, JM, my children and my new awareness of spirituality.

I love my mom with every fiber of my being. I have always loved my momma. I know that my momma is still with me. I know that my momma's love is everlasting. I know that my momma's spirit will be waiting for me; and for these reasons, I have peace. I will keep living.

I will always love you with all of my heart and I will always honor you mommy.

Peace, Love, and Light.

About the Author

FlightsInStilettos® was founded in 2018 by aspiring author, Kinyatta E. Gray based on her real-life travel style -- traveling glamorously through the airport. Kinyatta's goal is to inspire women travelers to put their best selves forward when traveling and to think about their individual travel style. Since launching FlightsInStilettos®, the signature t-shirts and travel accessories have been spotted around the world. "Travel, Glamour, Slay."

Acquiring success in the masses, FlightsInStilettos® has truly taken off. This year, FlightsInStilettos® debuted during New York Fashion Week and was spotted being worn by a host of celebrities. The celebs that supported the honor tote by FlightsInStilettos® include fashion influencer Maui Bigelow, celebrity make-up artist Nydia Figueroa , MTV Wild ' N ' Out and Trl, Davida D, Bravo's "Blood Sweat & Heels" Kim Dillinger, IHeart radio show host Madison Jaye and Youtuber Ifueko Igbinovia. FlightsInStilettos® travel accessories have also been supported by the Bravo network "Housewives of New Jersey & New York's" Delores Catania and Sonja Morgan, as well as Housewives of Potomac's Karen Huger.

In addition, FlightsInStilettos® was featured on noted top tier websites such as Buzzfeed and ThriveGlobal. Adding to their success, they have been featured on vast platforms such as Medium, Love Thy Self, The Bunnie Hole, Spillin The Tea, On Mogul and Madisonjaye.com. In addition, FlightsInStilettos® have been highlighted in publications such as Vine Magazine, LWL Magazine, Authority Magazine and ENSPIRE Magazine.

FlightsInStilettos® has been worldly recognized by vast platforms. Rising in the brand's success, FlightsInStilettos® was featured in Fashion GXD Magazine, which was advertised on Amazon.com and Barnes & Nobles. FlightsInStilettos® was highlighted on the "Travel in Style" segment of BMORE Lifestyle on MyTV24 Baltimore co-anchored by Chardelle Moore & Christina Denny. In addition to being featured in editorials and television, the brand was introduced by Always Ask Asia of Radio One, Majic 102.3 & 92.7 during an "Introducing FlightsInStilettos®" segment. This was followed by an interview with DJ KeiTouch, also at Radio One, on The Outlet News and Entertainment Connection on 1450 & 95.9 News Talk during the "Black Brands" segment.

My beloved and cherished mother **Beverly Esther Carroll** suddenly departed this life on October 21, 2018. She was a lovely, talented, funny, respected and honorable Godly woman who was called home way too soon.

She was also a phenomenal singer and my **biggest FlightsInStilettos®** supporter and fan. She'd always be the first person to try out my new products, use them, promote them, talk about them, share them via Facebook and give me valuable feedback about each product.

My mother was my everything and will continue to be. She inspired me to believe in myself and to take this big leap. I believed in myself because she believed in me first.

My mother always talked about her missions trip to Kenya in 2005. She went to Kenya and worked with orphaned and abandoned children firsthand and developed a heart for them since she herself was an orphan.

I MADE IT TO A TIMES SQUARE BILLBOARD IN NYC!!!

Who would have thought that after a fun filled vacation with friends and tossing out a whimsical handle - "FlightsInStilettos®" would result in the creation of a brand that has been spotted globally, and a billboard feature in Times Square NYC?

When I tell you that anything that you set your mind to is possible, it is! I started out as a single mom of two kids, although I have always worked, I also survived with the help of daycare vouchers and rental assistance about 20 years ago.

Once I decided that I wanted something different for my life, I made the necessary choices and strategically planned out a better future.

FlightsInStilettos® was something that happened. I never planned to be a brand creator or a business owner. But there was something about FlightsInStilettos® that seemed to embody all of the things that make me unique. That was the beginning of how I monetized my life. If I can do it, so can you. If I can make it to Times Square, so can you. You just have to set your mind to, let go of anything holding you back, surround yourself with people who wish to elevate and inspire and you must stay FOCUSED.

Go and become legendary!

SHARE THIS BOOK!
ORDER MORE COPIES

Retail Price $12.99

Special Quantity Discounts

5-100 Books	$8.95 each
100-999 Books	$5.95 each
1000+ Books	$3.95 each

To place a bulk order, please email
flightsinstilettos@gmail.com

Books Published By Pen Legacy Publishing

Journals/Guides

Boss Moves Start with You: 2018 Self-Reflection Journal & Vision Planner by Briana McKnight

Maximizing Your Tax Refund Made Easy! by Khristina Barnes

2018 Legacy Journal & Planner: A Planning Tool for your Freedom & Future by Charron Monaye

Secure Your Legacy Journal by Charron Monaye

Book Anthologies

Bruised, Broken, and Blessed: Life Changing Stories That Will Ignite Hope, Elevate Personal Growth, and Confirm Your Greatness compiled by Charron Monaye & Shontaye Hawkins

Get Out of Your Own Way: Overcoming Adversity to Live In Your Truth Out Loud compiled by Charron Monaye

Get Out of Your Own Way: 11 Life-Changing Stories on How to Face Everything & Rise!

Get Out of Your Own Way: 11 Game-Changing Stories on Mastering the Power of Trust, Faith & Success

Inspirational/Non-Fiction

Respect Your Choices: Finding Balance in Success by Vaughn McNeill

Let Me Tell You Like I Told Myself: Love's Truth Never Changes by Summer Willow Fitch

The Power of Shut Up by Lisa Dove Washington

Santify Your Money: The 11th Commandment by Toni Moore

Beautiful Toxicity: Ontaria Kim Wilson

STOP Asking for Permission & Give Notice: How to Accept & Attain Who You Are Without Validation by Charron Monaye

Love the Real You: Uncovering Your "WHY" & Affirming You're Enough by Charron Monaye

Parenting/Caregiver

From CAREFREE to CAREGIVER: A 31-Day Devotional to Balance, Encourage, and Support You in Your New Role by Teraleen Campbell

Health/Wellness

Don't Give Up Too Soon: 10 Ways to Help You ReSET Your Energy, Mindset, Wellness & Tranquility by Tinesha Boswell

Entrepreneurial /Business

I Want To Quit My Job: 8 Entrepreneurial Strategies For Massive Results While Employed

Fiction

Leonard Smith by AJ Harrison

MisLeading Lady by Sharon Y. Judie

Memoirs
The Black Blood in My Heart by La'Mena Marie
The Shadow in My Eyes by Deborah Rose
The Woodshed by Jaguar Wright
How I Survived Without Chemotherapy: One Woman's Story from Diagnosed to Thriving by Sabrina Moore
Stop Being a Doormat & Start Being a Boss by Toni Moore
Confidence Unlocked by Kiawana Key

Books are available on Amazon, Barnes N Noble, Books A Million, Wal-Mart, Penlegacy.com

www.ingramcontent.com/pod-product-compliance
Lightning Source LLC
Chambersburg PA
CBHW061223070526
44584CB00029B/3963